# EVERGLADES NATIONAL PARK

A TRUE BOOK

by

**Wende Fazio**

## Children's Press®
A Division of Grolier Publishing

New York  London  Hong Kong  Sydney
Danbury, Connecticut

*Reading Consultant*
**Linda Cornwell**
*Learning Resource Consultant*
*Indiana Department*
*of Education*

**Author's Dedication**
*To Aunt Nancy and*
*Uncle Mike*

**The park's entrance**

**Visit Children's Press® on the Internet at:**
**http://publishing.grolier.com**

Library of Congress Cataloging-in-Publication Data

Fazio, Wende.
    Everglades National Park / by Wende Fazio.
        p.   cm. — (A True book)
    Includes bibliographical references and index.
    Summary: Describes the history, landscape, wildlife, and activities for
visitors at Everglades National Park.
    ISBN: 0-516-20667-2 (lib.bdg.)  0-516-26433-8 (pbk.)
    1. Everglades National Park (Fla.)—Juvenile literature.  [1. Everglades
National Park (Fla.) 2. National parks and reserves.]  I. Title. II. Series.
F317.E9F39   1998
975.9'39—dc21                                                    97-24127
                                                                     CIP
                                                                      AC

# Contents

Grassy Waters                                    5

The Story of the Everglades                      8

The Two Seasons                                 16

A Safe Place for Birds and Wildlife             20

Plants of the Everglades                        28

Protecting the Everglades                       36

To Find Out More                                44

Important Words                                 46

Index                                           47

Meet the Author                                 48

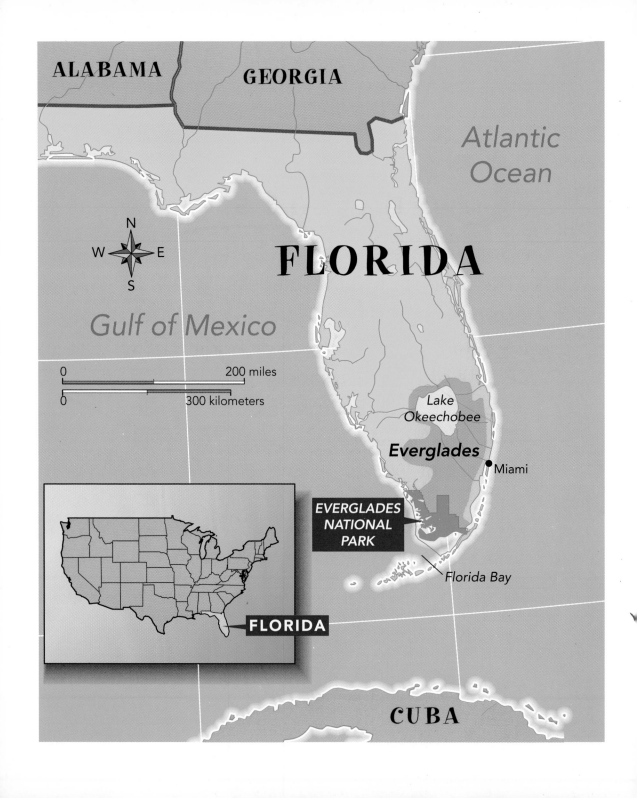

ALABAMA

GEORGIA

Atlantic
Ocean

FLORIDA

Gulf of Mexico

N
W   E
S

0                200 miles
0               300 kilometers

Lake
Okeechobee

*Everglades*

Miami

EVERGLADES
NATIONAL
PARK

Florida Bay

FLORIDA

CUBA

# Grassy Waters

Everglades National Park covers more than 1 million acres (about 1 million hectares) of land in the Florida Everglades. The Everglades is located in south Florida. It is made up of saw-grass prairies, mangrove swamps, and the warm waters of Florida Bay.

A view of Everglades
National Park

6

American Indians called this area, "Pa-Hay-Okee," or "grassy waters."

Millions of years ago, the Everglades was an ancient sea bottom. Today, it remains a low, flat area. The highest point in the Everglades is only 8 feet (2 meters) above sea level. The solid ground, or bedrock, is made up of limestone. Limestone is formed from the remains of sea shells and coral.

# The Story of the Everglades

The first American Indian people to live in the Everglades were called the "People of the Glades." They lived in permanent villages and hunted small mammals and deer. They built wooden canoes and caught large fish.

American Indians participate in a religious ceremony in their village.

In the 1500s, the Spanish were the first white settlers to arrive in south Florida. They wanted to convert the Indians to Christianity, and to settle the lands for Spain's king.

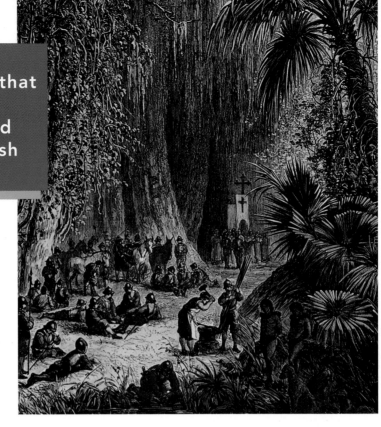

The first Europeans that the Indians encountered were Spanish explorers.

They also went to Florida to search for gold.

The Spanish built many missions and forts along the Florida coast. The Indians there were angry with the white settlers for taking their land. They attacked the Spanish forts and missions. But by 1800, there was only a handful of Indians left. Many of them had been captured by

A Seminole village in the Everglades

the Spanish and sold as slaves. Many more died from small-pox and other diseases. The Spanish soon left, and south Florida was then inhabited by the Muskogee Creek people. These people moved to south Florida from the areas that are now the Carolinas, Georgia, and Alabama. They became known as Seminole. Today, the relatives of these Seminole still live within Everglades National Park.

Large birds, such as blue herons (left) and great white egrets (above), were hunted almost to extinction.

In the early 1900s, south Florida was raided by hunters. Some of the hunters killed large birds for their colorful feathers. Thousands of birds were killed before the hunting

Royal Palm State Park got its name from the royal palm trees found through-out the area.

was stopped. Several types of birds came close to extinction (dying out forever) because of these hunters.

In 1916, a small area of the Everglades was given protection from hunters. It became Royal Palm State Park. In 1931, the United States Congress passed a bill to protect most of south Florida. On December 6, 1947, President Harry S. Truman dedicated Everglades National Park.

# The Two Seasons

The Everglades has two seasons. They are the wet season (summer) and the dry season (winter).

The summer rains begin in May or June. Afternoon thunderstorms turn the saw-grass prairies bright green. As much as 10 to 12 inches (25 to 30

Many people prefer to visit Everglades National Park during the dry season.

centimeters) of rain can fall in a single day during the summer!

In November, the water begins to seep into the ground and over the land toward Florida Bay. The dry season is coming. The green saw-grass

Saw grass as it looks during the wet summer season (above). The lack of water during the dry season turns the saw grass gold and brown (right).

shoots turn gold and dry up. The water recedes, or moves back, and settles into ponds and gator holes.

# Gator Holes

As winter approaches, the alligator begins a special project. With feet, tail, and snout, the alligator churns and thrashes in the soft ground until it has created a large hole. This "gator hole" slowly fills with water. It attracts many animals because water is not easy to find in the winter. But under the water, the alligator is waiting. It eats the small animals that wander to the hole for a drink.

A baby alligator rides on its mother's back.

# A Safe Place for Birds and Wildlife

The Everglades is home to many types of wading birds. Wading birds are long-legged shore birds that walk through shallow water and marshes looking for food. The great egret, snowy egret, and roseate spoonbill are

The great egret (left) and roseate spoonbill (right) are two kinds of wading birds that can be found at Everglades National Park.

wading birds that can be seen throughout the park.

The anhinga is sometimes called the snakebird because

it swims through the water with only its thin neck showing. You can watch anhingas dive for fish. They never seem to miss!

The wood stork is the only stork native to the United States. These birds have large bills. They hunt for fish by swimming underwater with their bills open. When a fish bumps into the open bill, the wood stork snaps its bill shut in an instant!

Anhingas (above) have webbed feet to help them swim, and sharp bills to spear fish. The wood stork (right) stands about 4 feet (1 meter) tall.

The bald eagle (above) is found only in North America, and is the national bird of the United States. A snail kite (right) prepares to eat the snail it is holding in its beak

Bald eagles and snail kites are other kinds of birds that are at home in the Everglades. Bald eagles are endangered. This means that they are in danger of becoming extinct. Snail kites have a wingspan of more than 3 feet (1 m).

The American alligator is the Everglades's most famous resident. The male alligator can grow to 16 feet (5 m) or longer. The alligator is a cold-blooded reptile. It needs to

Two alligators warm themselves in the hot Florida sun.

lie in the sun to warm up its body enough to move around. An alligator will eat anything it can catch. If you see one, be sure to keep a safe distance away!

Crocodiles grow to about 12 feet (4 meters) long.

The American crocodile is similar to the American alligator, but there are differences between them that you can look for. The crocodile has a smaller snout. It is also lighter in color.

# Plants of the Everglades

Much of the Everglades is covered with saw grass. Saw grass is a kind of grass that grows in water. Its edges are made up of tiny, sharp teeth. Saw grass doesn't need much water to grow in. The water beneath the saw grass is only about 6 inches (15 cm) deep.

Saw grass grows in abundance throughout Everglades National Park.

The red, peeling bark of the gumbo-limbo tree reminds many people of a peeling sunburn.

Trees such as oak, mahogany, and the gumbo-limbo tree, grow throughout the Everglades. The colorful gumbo-limbo tree has been nicknamed the "tourist tree." This is because its peeling red bark looks like a visitor who has stayed out in the Florida sun too long!

The strangler fig grows on other trees. The strangler fig begins as a seed. The seed plants itself in another tree, called a host tree. As the seed grows, it drops long roots to the ground. It begins to twist itself around its host's

A strangler fig grows around the trunk of a cypress tree.

trunk. Eventually, the host
tree is strangled and dies.
The air plant also grows
on other plants, but doesn't

harm them. It gets all the water and food it needs from the air. The wild orchids of Everglades National Park are examples of air plants.

Although their flowers have not yet bloomed, these wild orchids are growing on the trunk of a tree.

The slash pine is a hardy tree that has pine cones. It is able to put roots down in almost no soil at all.

The mangrove tree lives in a swampy mixture of both

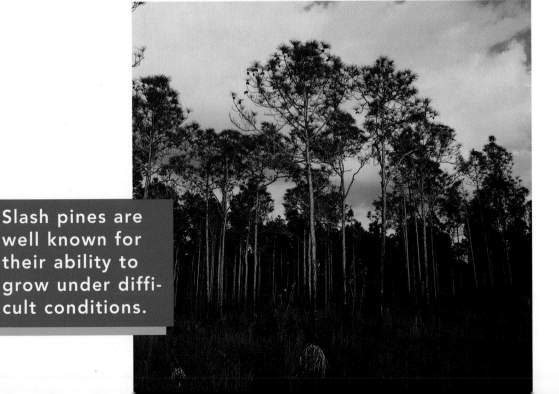

Slash pines are well known for their ability to grow under difficult conditions.

Here, you can clearly see the prop roots of red mangrove trees.

land and water. Red, black, white, and buttonwood mangroves grow in the Everglades. Mangroves stand up on several roots that spread out from their trunk. These roots are called prop roots. They bend down to take hold in the muck below.

# Protecting the Everglades

Everglades National Park, and the entire Everglades, is a unique natural environment. But the area is in trouble. The Everglades depends on nearby Lake Okeechobee to supply it with fresh, clean water. However, the lake has been dammed many times. There is less freshwater

Lake Okeechobee is the largest lake in Florida.

for the plants and animals of the Everglades. Also, saltwater from the Gulf of Mexico has reached farther inland than ever before. The saltwater has mixed with the freshwater of the Everglades. This has hurt

Efforts are being made to protect threatened animals, such as bobcats (above) and Florida panthers (right).

the area's delicate ecological balance. Many of the larger animals, including the bobcat, the panther, and the Florida bear, are now threatened with extinction. Many of the wading birds and alligators are shrinking in numbers.

Everglades National Park is home to more plants and animals facing possible extinction than any other park in the United States. But many people are working to protect the area. The U.S. government created the Endangered Species Act of 1973. This gave some protection to the ecology of the Everglades. In 1989, the Everglades National Park Protection and Expansion

Act was signed by President George Bush. This bill authorized the addition of 107,000 acres (43,000 hectares) to Everglades National Park. As a result, more of the Everglades became protected.

When you visit the Everglades, your visit will be more enjoyable if you remember a few rules: Stay on marked trails, and follow your national park service guide. Don't approach wildlife. Don't take any plants or grass away

Although these visitors (above) are enjoying their encounter with an alligator, they are standing much too close to it. This is an aerial view of Everglades National Park (right).

with you when you leave. It's up to everyone to help protect one of the United States's national treasures.

# Endangered Everglades

**H**uman development has caused much of the native wildlife in the Everglades to lose their habitats (the lands they live on). Endangered species are close to extinction. Here are six endangered species found in the Everglades and southern Florida:

*American crocodile* → There are only a few hundred crocodiles in southern Florida. Just a few dozen of them are actively breeding.

← *Florida manatee* This gentle mammal lives in Florida's warm, tropical waters. It grows up to 13 feet (4 m) long and weighs as much as 2,000 pounds (900 kilograms). Their numbers have been reduced to about 1,200.

# Species of National Park

➜ *Florida panthers* are believed to be the only panther living in the eastern United States. Florida law has protected it from hunters since 1966. Today, this graceful cat is endangered by shrinking habitat and highway traffic.

*Schaus swallowtail* This brightly colored, yellow-and-brown butterfly is found only in the hardwood trees of some of the Florida Keys. Its habitat is also getting smaller.

*Snail kite* The snail kite is now one of the rarest birds in the United States. Fewer than 1,000 are believed to exist in Florida.

⬅ *Sea turtles* Five species of sea turtles live in the tropical waters around the Everglades. They are endangered as a result of hunters, destruction or removal of their eggs, and loss of their nesting areas.

# To Find Out More

Here are some additional resources to help you learn more about Everglades National Park:

 **Books**

Brown, Mary Barrett. **Wings along the Waterway.** Orchard Books, 1992.

Cooper, Jason. **The Everglades.** Rourke Press, 1995.

Fradin, Dennis B. **Florida.** Children's Press, 1992.

George, Jean Craighead. **Everglades.** HarperCollins, 1995.

Lourie, Peter. **Buffalo Tiger and the River of Grass.** Boyds Mills Press, 1994.

# Organizations and Online Sites

**Everglades National Park**
40001 State Road #9336
Homestead, FL 33034-6733
*http://taz.interpoint.net/*
*~ahs/cyberfair96/glades/*
*table.htm*

**Friends of the Everglades**
7800 Red Road
Suite 215K
Miami, Florida 33143

**Great Outdoor Recreation Pages (GORP)**
*http://www.gorp.com/*
*resource/US_National_Park/*
*main.htm*

Information on hiking, fishing, boating, climate, places to stay, plant life, wildlife, and more.

**National Park Foundation**
1101 17th Street N.W.
Suite 1008
Washington, D.C. 20036

Compuserve offers online maps, park products, special programs, and in-depth information that is available by park name, state, region, or interest. From the main menu, select Travel, then Where To Go, then Complete Guide to America's National Parks.

**National Park Service**
Office of Public Inquiries
P. O. Box 37127
Washington, D.C. 20240
*http://www.nps.gov/*

**National Parks and Conservation Association**
1776 Massachusetts Ave.
 N.W.
Washington, D.C. 20036
*http://www.npca@npca.org*

# Important Words

*hardy* tough, able to survive under difficult conditions

*mission* headquarters for a group of people who teach their religion to others with different beliefs

*native* animal or plant that originally lived or grew in a certain place

*prairie* large area of level or rolling grassland

*sea level* the surface of the ocean

*smallpox* virus that causes high fever and skin bumps

*wingspan* the distance between the outer tips of the wings of a bird

# Index

(**Boldface** page numbers
   indicate illustrations.)

air plant, 32, 33, **33**
alligators, 19, **19,** 25, 26,
   **26,** 27, 39, **41**
American Indians, 7, 8, 9,
   **9,** 10, **10, 11**
birds, 13, **13,** 15, 20, 21,
   **21,** 22, **23, 24,** 25, 39,
   43
bobcat, 38, **38**
crocodiles, 27, **27,** 42, **42**
dry season (winter), 16,
   17, **17, 18,** 19
Everglades, 5, 7, 8, **11,**
   15, 16, 20, 25, 28, 30,
   35, 36, 37, 39, 40, 42
Florida, 5, 9, 10, 12, 13,
   15, 31, 42, 43
Florida Bay, 5, 17
Florida manatee, 42, **42**
Florida panther, 38, **38,**
   43, **43**
gator holes, 18, 19

gumbo-limbo tree, 30,
   **30,** 31
host tree, 31, 32
hunters, 13, 15, 43
Lake Okeechobee, 36, **37**
mangroves, 5, 34, 35, **35**
People of the Glades.
   *See* American Indians
prop roots, 35, **35**
Royal Palm State Park,
   **14,** 15
saw grass, 5, 16, 17, **18,**
   28, **29**
sea turtles, 43, **43**
Seminole. *See* American
   Indians
settlers, 9, 11
slash pine, 34, **34**
strangler fig, 31, **32**
tourist tree. *See* gumbo-
   limbo tree
United States, 15, 22, 39,
   41, 43
wet season (summer),
   16, 17, **18**

# Meet the Author

Wende Fazio's love for America's national parks began when she drove cross-country and back again from New Jersey. On that trip, she fell in love with the awesome beauty and vast wilderness of the many national parks of the West. She has since fallen in love with the national parks of the East. Acadia National Park, in Maine, and Everglades National Park are particularly special to her. Ms. Fazio and her husband John spend all of their free time hiking and photographing the national parks and wilderness areas of America.

Wende has written several books about a variety of subjects. She is also the author of *Acadia National Park* (True Books) for Children's Press.